SCHALK'S LITTLE BOOK OF COMBATIVE PRINCIPLES

Turn any martial art into a true combatives system.

Schalk Holloway

ISBN FOR PRINT EDITION: 9798774095247
Imprint: Independently Published

Cover design by: Schalk Willem Holloway

*Dedicated to all of those combative and martial arts
practitioners that are truly seeking mastery.*

ACKNOWLEDGEMENTS

A sincere thank you to Misters Terry Trahan, Mike "Ronin" Keller, Dragan Milojevic, and Gavin Coleman for taking the time to proof read and help me tighten up what is already a concise treatment. English is not my first language. I speak it fairly well but I still think in Afrikaans. Your help and guidance is much appreciated.

CONTENTS

INTRODUCTION

A while ago I mentioned to a friend in the States that, traditionally, we as South Africans were quite cut off from good learning material when it came to self-defense and combatives. As I get older and I dig around I find that there is amazing content, specifically in the form of print and video media, from the 1990's and earlier. During those years, however, our country was globally isolated, facing a tremendous amount of trade sanctions. The odds of those books or videos landing here were extremely small. Moving into the 21st century, especially with the proliferation of blogs on the internet, access slowly started to open up. Gone were the days of having to rely on the traditional martial arts for self-defense - we could finally catch up on all things combatives! From here I started reading, quite avidly, voices like Marc MacYoung, Rory Miller, Wim De Meere, and Loren Christensen, to name but a few. Which brings me to my point, albeit in a slightly roundabout way:

As I'm getting older, and as I'm discovering some of that pre-21st century material, I'm consistently reminded that there simply isn't very much that's new under the sun.

I say this from a desire to be a person of integrity: I firmly believe that many of the principles in this book, or at least, parts of their application can be found in others' earlier work. Just the other day, I found a post on Facebook concerning the combative principles of attachment and adhesion (which one of the proof readers says he first came across in the work of the late Bob Orlando). These principles dovetail quite a bit with my principle of Positive Contact as described in this Little Book. This is tremendously comforting as it serves as an external verification point to what I've discovered on my own journey.

Does this mean you can only expect a regurgitation of what's already available out there? No, I sincerely don't think so. The book is structured in such a way that the principles make systemic sense. That means you will be able to use them to shape whatever you are currently doing in a more combative direction irrespective of your point of departure. Obviously I am a product of my own training, experience, and background, but I'm also confident in my unique method of thorough thinking and development. I'm positive that you will find value in this treatment.

I warn you, however, like all my books this one won't be easy to digest, either. I'm confident that I write in a legible (thanks to my proof-readers) and understandable manner, but all my books require that you also do your own thinking and development to integrate what you have learned into your journey. It's been interesting to see that, and I say this respectfully, lazy or recreational readers occasionally struggle with my work. They are either there for "the next best thing" (lazy reader) or simply for an enjoyable experience (recreational reader); there are people in both of these categories that struggle with my work as they didn't necessarily sign up for the post-reading effort required for integration. No hard feelings with either, though, as long as I can add some value I'm content.

Lastly, let me add the following: the reason the principles are in parenthesis is that these principles are literally what gets repeated verbally, including frequently being screamed and shouted, to and at our clients. Over and over and over we repeat these principles to them. We teach on them, we coach on them, we reflect and debrief on them, we even discipline on them. These are the principles that drive everything we do. Yes, from my personal training and experience background, we have our technique and procedure sets that we teach our clients but those are simply the tools in the toolbox. Everything we do is based on these principles and we make sure to drive them consistently, purposefully, and hard through all of our training spaces.

My wish, as always, is that this book provides immense value to your own combative journey. Enjoy.

PART 1

3 IMPORTANT CONTEXTUAL CONSIDERATIONS

THE CLOSE COMBAT INCIDENT & COMBATIVES

It's important to revisit, or for some, to try and establish, a working definition of a close combat incident (hereinafter mostly referred to as a CCI) due to the following axiom:

The purpose of combatives are to assist in the resolution of a close combat incident.

Combatives, as both an approach to martial arts as well as individual techniques, should be selected and deployed purposefully to assist in resolving a close combat incident. Thus, it is important to define what such an incident is so that we can better understand combatives within its macro context. In The Maul Book we described it as:

An incident that occurs within arms length, and that requires a combative application of force to resolve. It may be defensive or offensive in nature.

Holloway, Schalk; Coleman, Gavin. The Maul: Preparing for the Chaos of Close Combatives (p. 5). Kindle Edition.

In unpacking this definition we can add the following in relation to combatives:

An incident that occurs within arms length.

Range is one of the primary drivers of tactics and, as such, also key in selecting the tools, techniques, and procedures required to reach certain outcomes. In The Maul Book we focused mostly on hand to hand and shorter edged and pointed weapons; however, it is not necessarily that combatives are only focused on these weapon categories. Combatives might be deployed alongside firearms, as well as through the use of other cold (non firing, as in not firearms in this context) weapons. Irrespective of the weapon type or platform, the one primary determining factor for the use of combatives is a close range. We define this range as being within arms length for ease of use and remembrance, it might however be slightly longer when considering certain cold weapons.

That requires a combative application of force to resolve.

A good leading question to unpacking this point would be the following: why are we referring specifically to a *combative* application of force? A close combat incident is any incident where we are attempting to use the application of force, in the sense of mass times acceleration, to make an individual or group of individuals do something against their will. Combatives are specifically deployed to control, detain, hurt and/or damage others with the goal of getting them to start or stop doing something that is not their intention to start or stop doing. Understanding that all violence is inherently complex, extremely dynamic, and therefore mostly has unpredictable outcomes, the goal should also be to force this compliance as fast as possible and, in doing so, limit potential for injury to the practitioner or his team mates. Combatives, as well as their respective tactics, tools, techniques, and procedures should be selected in line with this primary requirement of fast resolution.

Defensive or offensive in nature.

Whereas a close combat incident might be defensive or offensive in nature, combatives are neutral. Combatives should be effective within both defensive or offensive situations. There might be specific combatives selected within certain scenarios, but this would be purely because they would be more apt to accomplish whatever next outcome is required. There is, and should be, no differentiation between defensive or offensive combatives. Combatives are simply tools deployed to accomplish a specific goal within the moment.

THE NECESSITY OF PROCESS MINDEDNESS

Seeing as we are deploying combatives to resolve an incident, it then stands to reason we need to treat an incident correctly. Let's consider certain principles:

Any incident, including a close combat incident, is a process with a start and a finish.

Many practitioners, if not expressed verbally but in their training, approach incidents as events with only one segment or stage. They isolate, what might be valid, individual segments of a complete CCI and then train responses to them as separate techniques. Consider, if you will, certain Krav Maga and close combat systems, training an isolated weapon disarm or a strike defense and response. I've frequently seen this type of practitioner fall apart within pressure testing as well as actual CCIs. CCIs are highly dynamic - everything is constantly changing. In a certain sense the CCI is a storm to be navigated; the CCI is in charge and it's the job of the practitioner to ride it out as effectively and efficiently as possible. A practitioner should be able to navigate this dynamism by deploying combatives, moment to moment, as and when and where the CCI requires them to be deployed. Our use of combatives should thus allow us to effectively and efficiently navigate a CCI from the start, right through all the messy bits in the middle, to the finish.

Always aim to resolve the CCI as early in the process as possible.

Bearing the above principle in mind, we don't need a mindset which drags out the process unnecessarily. If it is possible to select combatives which will allow us to resolve the CCI sooner then we should do so. Also, any combatives selected should still drive us towards our required outcome, that is to say, we should still finish where we intended to finish. As one becomes more proficient, there is usually an opportunity to shorten the duration of the middle segment of the CCI. Practically, this means that the effectiveness of a technique selected and deployed at a specific stage of the process may actually complete the whole process for us. For example, an Entry strike that actually knocks the opponent down and unconscious allowing the practitioner to immediately arrest or, as another example, consider a Takedown applied forcefully enough that it provides immediate compliance for whatever Finish the practitioner needs to apply.

This mindset is also of import when considering training methodologies and/or practice drills. For example, consider trapping (Holloway, Schalk; Coleman, Gavin. The Maul: Preparing for the Chaos of Close Combat (p. 92). Kindle Edition.) or variations of the sticky hands drill (kindly consult Google or your instructors). These drills are excellent in terms of providing volume of repetition or volume of variation when it comes to practice. However, their inherent structure leads to drawn out engagement. We use some of these drills as cornerstones of our training, but we ensure to balance them out with others that ingrain the mindset of efficient resolution of the CCI.

We always fight until we're done.

Here we come to the fundamental issue: all of our training and practice should empower us to continue fighting until we have reached an intended outcome. If we don't treat the CCI as a process we run the immense risk of not completing this objective. We might start strong but falter in the middle. We might do reasonably well during the middle portion of a CCI and then run out of gas or options towards the end. We might reach the finish but have no idea what to do with the Opponent - think in terms of detainment, arrest, or kill - once we arrive there. The mindset of the professional practitioner should be clear and focused: they need to understand their intended outcome clearly and then be able to manage the process to that end. When we don't treat a CCI as a process this will be impossible.

THE COMBATIVE TRIAD
Speed, Surprise and Violence of Action

VIOLENCE OF
ACTION

The triangle above is an illustration of what is frequently referred to, at least in the spheres in which I find myself, as "The Three Principles of Combat". It's important to note, though, that this triangle is widely known by different monikers and, at times, with a slight variation on the one element. Whereas Speed and Violence of Action are usually constant, Surprise is sometimes replaced by Accuracy (largely in the shooting community). This triangle has its roots in modern CQB (or CQC) from where it has been, quite liberally in my opinion, transplanted into other combat, self-defense, and combative contexts. When I say, quite liberally, I don't mean this in the sense of it being purely or completely negative. These three principles or elements of CQB, within certain contexts, are required and sensible. However, once one changes the context, certain interpretations and applications of these principles may become problematic. This relates primarily to the fact that the ROE (Rules of Engagement) and outcomes, and as such, tactics, differ vastly between the fields of combat and civilian life. It's also important to understand that apart from general special powers of arrest, as well as certain liberties provided to special teams or task forces within certain law enforcement environments, most regular security, police, and law enforcement officers essentially function within much of the same legal constraints as do regular civilians. It should be obvious then that one should be careful to not blindly apply principles of combat to civilian, or even regular security, police, or law enforcement contexts.

To be honest, I was slightly hesitant to add this chapter to this treatment. Two reasons apply: first, I believe that a full treatment of this topic might be worth a book on its own. That said, however, simply touching on these issues should be enough to at least inspire some thought in the reader. Second, this triangle seems to be a holy cow in certain combative environments. It's very closely coupled to the ego of certain instructors as well as to the sense of bravado certain groups try and cultivate within their communities. Thus, touching on it in too a concise manner might be insufficient to thoroughly argue its case. Anyway, that said, let's attempt a very brief treatment.

Bear in mind the purpose is to create a set of principles that would be effective in all contexts.

Violence of Action vs. Appropriate Force

Violence of Action is simply the use of overwhelming force. However, overwhelming force can be interpreted both as *as much force as can be generated within a specific context* or, as *using just enough force to ensure a specific outcome*. For the civilian or law enforcement officer it might be the difference between, for example:

• Shooting an attacker even after they've stopped or have disengaged from the attack, or just shooting an attacker until the attack stops.

• Continuing to kick an opponent that's already down and unconscious, or only using combatives to stop the attack and then disengaging.

- Breaking a joint during a detain and arrest, or simply applying enough pain to force compliance.

Now this might sound like common sense, and to some of us it is, the problem, though, is with the mindset ingrained in the training environment. Conditioning someone in the traditional sense of Violence of Action, within the wrong context, allows them to open a door that becomes very difficult to close. Let me provide two anecdotal examples, both from my own personal experience:

I remember how, during a drug raid in a dark but public space, I forcefully removed what turned out to be an elderly lady from a truck with darkened windows. I violently threw her onto a tar parking bay and proceeded to keep her pinned to the floor until a team mate took control of her. This all happened within seconds and was purely bad luck for her as she, and one other male, were seated in a vehicle directly opposite the vehicle we were busting. Unfortunately for them, they looked like they were part of the target's surveillance team. In all honesty, and talking from experience, I had other options in that moment which I didn't take due to the Violence of Action conditioning.

Another example was from a raid we did alongside one of our South African special task forces. The area of the raid was quite contained apart from a section immediately across from the target area. This area had a small group of males that couldn't be evacuated. One of these males, a youngster with a bit of an attitude problem, was taking video on his cellphone after being instructed not to. One of the task force team members proceeded to ask the youngster for his phone so that the media can be deleted. The youngster proceeded to get slightly cocky and the team member responded by assaulting him and forcefully confiscating the phone. Without going into details, let me just say a disproportionate and unnecessary amount of force was used to reach the outcome.

Essentially it is an issue of whether the force application has any brakes on it or not. One can argue that the fault in the two anecdotes above lie with the operator, but the operator is largely the product of his or her training. When simply conditioning Violence of Action it'll be difficult to apply any brakes. Now again, this is necessary within certain contexts but most definitely out of place in most others. Appropriate Force can be up-scaled to Violence of Action but Violence of Action struggles to be down-scaled to Appropriate Force. Better then, both in my opinion and in that of many other training programs, to teach good rapid decision making coupled with the application of Appropriate Force under stressful conditions.

The quick discussion above should highlight the essence of the shift in thinking. The idea is to try and replace the principle with one that offers a wider range of options and then to adapt training methods to it. To avoid labouring the point (and stay within the Little Book parameters) I'm only going to provide short and essential arguments for the next two principles.

Speed vs. Purposeful Movement

Speed, in the same manner as Violence of Action, should also be adapted to the immediate context and to certain other factors as well. Our assumption is that high speed is always good. However, if we have to consider, for example, searching a building with the intention of clearing possible hostiles, speed of movement would actually vary according to team size. If there was a large team, flooding a room might be appropriate. If there is only a two man team, a slower but smooth limited penetration might be more appropriate.

The other important issue when considering speed relates to technical proficiency. Frequently highly proficient individuals and/or teams actually appear slightly slower than untrained or inexperienced ones. The main reason for this is efficiency of movement, coupled with better assessment and rapid decision making skills, in the proficient individual. Their base movement speed might be slower, but their execution is still faster. The untrained or inexperienced frequently push faster than necessary, their movement patterns might be jerky or rushed, even sacrificing certain critical fundamentals in the interest of speed.

When it comes to choosing speed of execution, we should rather consider elements like context and outcome, resources available, and technical proficiency, to name but a few critical ones; we should always be focusing on Purposeful Movement, meaning, the correct movement and speed as determined by these elements, rather than arbitrarily attempting to go fast.

Surprise / Accuracy vs. Good Tactics

Before continuing, I just want to note that whereas Surprise is a tactic, Accuracy is actually a skill. Therefore, the expectation should always be that a high level of Accuracy is developed and present. Considering Surprise, though, Surprise is obviously a good tactic as it provides and allows one to maintain initiative when used correctly. However, there are times where initiative might have been lost and where we now need to rely on other tactics. The argument then is that one will always need Good Tactics, one of which is Surprise. Once again, a thorough discussion on tactics is not the aim of this book and, as such, falls outside the scope of this treatment.

The Combative Triad

As we move into the next part of the book it's important to note that all 12 Combative Principles have been aligned with the changes suggested in this chapter. The items discussed in this chapter are very concise and only core thoughts specifically connected to the next part of the book were quickly touched on. The changes to the original model have been captured in what I call The Combative Triad, it forms the core reference point of most of our instruction. A schematic can be found below:

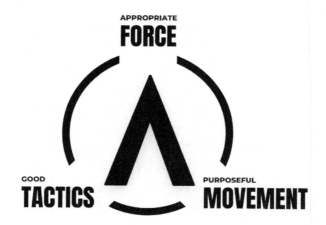

PART 2

12 COMBATIVE PRINCIPLES

"KNOW YOUR DESIRED OUTCOME."

The outcome should be determined by both the working context of the practitioner, as well as the immediate situation itself. Military, various forms of law enforcement and security workers, as well as civilians, all have different outcomes for a CCI. Whereas the military's first probable requirement is killing an enemy combatant or, at the very least, severely injuring said enemy combatant to the point of them not being able to reciprocate, law enforcement's will primarily be detainment and/or arrest. A security officer might have a wider range of outcomes ranging from possible use of lethal force, to detainment and/or arrest, to escorting or moving a combative individual to another locale, to simply reporting an incident or managing access to a site. Civilians, predominantly, simply need to escape alive and as unscathed as possible. However, as a CCI progresses, the dynamic situation might change and accordingly dictate a change in outcome. As a simple and accessible example, consider the self-defender initially trying to force a hole to escape but now finding themselves having to fight for their life.

Each of these differing outcomes will determine a myriad of other factors when it comes to the CCI; each and every other decision made within the engagement or CCI should be influenced by this principle. It should determine the amount and type of force applied, and it should determine the moment of disengagement, or, conversely, to what extent the practitioner remains engaged in the CCI. Largely, though, it should determine a very clear image of what the end of the CCI should be and look like. This is important conceptually, but also practically for two reasons: first of all, it will provide the driving direction during the CCI; and second, it will determine which techniques, as well as which final positions, if any, is required for detainment or arrest. Subsequently, these techniques and final positions then need extensive training and practice so that they ultimately become ingrained in the practitioner's toolset.

In The Maul, the combative approach I personally use, we have a fixed process for resolving CCIs. The last stage of the process is what we call Finish. Finish, for us, is a set of contextual options and positions (if any are required) that are aligned to the different outcomes. We spend just as much time training this Finishing stage as every other stage of the CCI. Whereas this Little Book is written to be generically useful, internally we refer to this principle as "know your finish." The practitioner is expected to have a clear understanding of where they are driving the CCI, what the Finish position looks like, and how to get there in a proficient manner.

"ASSESSMENT IS A PART OF THE PROCESS."

Assessment should continuously be present in all stages of an incident. That would be pre-incident, during the actual CCI, upon resolution of the CCI and, interestingly enough, even well after an incident has been resolved (as certain incidents have repercussions based on the incident's effect on the role-players). In a macro-sense, then, every stage of an incident should be started with an assessment. The type of assessment, meaning whether it's hasty or thorough, might be influenced by the situation's inherent dynamics, but the assessment itself can never be dropped from the process.

This is especially important to understand from a training perspective. How and where do we integrate different types of assessments into the training process? How do we ensure that an assessment has actually been done by the trainee or practitioner seeing as it's a mental process unobservable by the outside eye? This question needs to be explored by the instructors or developers of the training system or approach and done past the old cliché of the "security check", so prevalent in the firearms industry. It's one thing to integrate a left to right head movement pattern into a process, it's quite another thing to program the brain to accurately assess for key indicators and determinants during a dynamic process.

On a micro-scale or, that is, during the close combat phase of the incident itself, assessment should continuously be done in a cyclical manner. All decision making, whether consciously in System 2, or less consciously in System 1, should actually be preceded by an assessment. Boyd's OODA loop would call this the Observe and Orient phases preceding the Decision and Act phases. The quality of this continuous assessment directly impacts the quality of the proceeding decisions and execution. Training methodologies should be developed to program continuous assessment into the trainee's mental processes. When this is not done properly we usually notice three prevalent issues surfacing:

First, wrong combative techniques get selected for the required outcome. This primarily relates to selecting combatives that don't serve the current range dynamics; this, in turn, will have a negative cascading effect on force generation and application. The second issue with a lack of assessment, and especially if the practitioner has ingrained set movement patterns or combative combinations, is the delivery of techniques in directions or spaces where the opponent has already moved from (opponent simply isn't there anymore). You find this quite often in very commercial Krav Maga and close combat systems where the practitioner is taught to always give three knees to the groin, for example: sometimes the opponent simply moves and you find the practitioner striking into thin air. The last issue pertains to the practitioner continually attempting some technique or procedure which simply isn't working. However, instead of changing tactics they simply continue to try and muscle or force the ineffective technique to work. What's actually required is a hasty assessment on why the technique or procedure isn't working which, in so doing, will allow the practitioner to select a new technique or procedure that might be more effective.

All this sounds like common sense, 'If it's not working stop doing it.' However, if we don't intentionally program the brain to identify and make that judgment call accurately within the moment, then it simply won't. Incidentally, our primary method for dealing with this is the Control stage of our CCI Resolution Process. Good control provides safety in the moment, which in turn can be used to do proper assessments.

If we could spend one more moment on this last dynamic: I can't overstate how important it is to understand the current objective problem during the CCI. Many practitioners over-focus on weapons, first, and fast movements, second. This is understandable due to inherent risk in both of these factors; the brain is very much adapted to focus on these two. However, consider as example, an attacker grabbing your left shoulder, pulling you in tight, and stabbing you around and behind that left arm with his right arm. This is an old ambush tactic used in a wide variety of endemic settings, prison being the most prevalent. In that moment, yes, the knife is what's doing the damage, but, it's the opponent's left arm controlling you that is the real and current objective problem. If you don't deal with that control issue you won't be able to deal with the knife issue.

When training a practitioner to assess, we need to work with them to understand what the actual problem is that takes precedence within any moment. We should assist them in avoiding tunnel vision and help them to identify what problem needs to be solved, right now, so that we can further resolve the CCI.

"WHEN YOU ENTER IS JUST AS IMPORTANT AS HOW YOU ENTER."

This principle was originally sparked by a petite female client when she asked me "so when do I actually hit him?" This made me realise that we didn't have a sensible way of teaching our non-military clients how to make effective decisions concerning the issue. It's different within CQB environments as those are mostly (not always) pro-active clearing engagements with no civilian legal constraints. For most other contexts' the practitioner might find themselves in a significantly more reactive, as well as tactically inferior, posture after they realise they are in trouble. Correctly answering the question of "when" is a fundamental requirement when it comes to correctly managing potentially violent encounters: if I apply force too soon I can very easily find myself in legal trouble; if I apply force too late I can very easily find myself severely injured or worse. It is important then to have a reference for, and a method to determine, "when" exactly one should Enter.

For those not familiar with the terms Enter or Entry, we define an Entry as:

A technique used to close range.

Holloway, Schalk; Coleman, Gavin. The Maul: Preparing for the Chaos of Close Combatives (p. 6). Kindle Edition.

As such, an Entry can be any form of movement, strike, technique, force application etc. used to launch one's attack on the opponent. Essentially we are trying to determine the moment that I execute the Entry. We call this process of selecting the best Moment of Execution, "Trigger Setting". The Trigger being a mentally set qualifier that would indicate the exact Moment of Execution. Following is a concise description of the three primary Triggers that we employ:

Confirmation Trigger

The qualifier would be any action taken by the opponent that confirms them as a threat. Some examples may be: removing a weapon from a pocket, sheath, or holster; sudden displays of dominant behaviour indicating a limbic fight response; declaring intention to harm the practitioner; etc.

Opportunity Trigger

The qualifier would be any action taken by the opponent that breaks their focus and concentration away from the practitioner or, alternatively, that lessens or negates their ability to attack the practitioner. Some examples may be: the opponent looking away; removal of a trigger finger from a trigger guard; the opponent reaching down towards the practitioner's pockets; etc.

Necessity Trigger

The qualifier would be any action that gives the practitioner the conviction that the opponent is about to cause serious bodily harm or apply potentially lethal force. Some examples might be: the opponent, while having both the ability and opportunity, declaring to the practitioner that they are going to rape or kill him/her now; a second opponent instructing the primary to kill the practitioner; the opponent displaying specific and communicable behaviours which can be interpreted as intention to apply grievous bodily harm or lethal force; etc.

More can be found on this topic in The Maul: Preparing for the Chaos of Close Combat, written by myself and Gavin Coleman.

"ALWAYS KEEP TWO HANDS ON THE PROBLEM."

When facing hot weapons, that is weapons with a combustible component like firearms, the problem is the weapon itself. When facing cold weapons, that is blunt, edged, and/or pointed weapons, the problem is the weapon bearing limb. Why the limb with cold weapons? It should be obvious that we don't want to try and grab sharp or pointed objects moving at high velocity. In terms of blunt objects, however, we want to be efficient and have the same primary tactics and movement patterns across a broad spectrum of problems; we simply treat all cold weapons in the same manner.

Also, in terms of biomechanics, velocity increases and target size decreases distally in the limb. That is, the forearm travels faster and is smaller than the upper arm, and so does the hand in relation to the forearm; the weapon is usually faster but not necessarily smaller than the hand, and the tip of the weapon is obviously both the fastest and smallest target on the spectrum. Better then to aim the intervention upstream as the target will be both larger and slower moving.

It's also important to consider the opponent's reaction once we actually grab the problem. Predominantly, there's an initial jerking reaction. If you grab, for example, an opponent's pistol, they'll immediately jerk it backwards in reaction. For this reason, we always aim to have one hand behind the weapon if at all possible; in terms of a pistol, for example, we might try to get one hand on the slide and one behind the striker or the hammer. Techniques, however, should be robust enough that they'll still work if the dynamism of the CCI screws this up . For example, the grabbing technique should still work if we miss the rear of the pistol but manage to catch his hand or wrist instead.

There is an inordinate amount of risk in trying to control the problem with only one hand which, in my opinion, is not worth it or even necessary. A full discussion on these risks fall outside the scope of this treatment but I invite anyone to reach out and we can set up a proper communication channel in which I'll explain it thoroughly.

Back to the point: there will likely be an immediate jerking reaction when trying to grab an opponent's weapon or weapon-bearing limb. It is interesting to note the resistance pattern when grabbing the weapon or limb, usually it looks like this:

1. The opponent either immediately does or does not notice the restriction in movement. It's important to note that the opponent's brain doesn't initially interpret the restriction: things happen too fast in a dynamic CCI; it simply either notices the restriction, or it doesn't.

2. Once the restriction is noticed, however, there's an instinctive jerking reaction; the initial jerk might be followed by a couple of fast but underpowered jerking motions.

3. Then, at some stage, the opponent's brain catches up and realises that the weapon or limb is stuck; once the opponent realises the weapon or limb is stuck more powerful, aggressive, and violent dislodging movement patterns can be expected.

I always teach my clients to remember that we shouldn't be maintaining any position for a long time. Ideally, the two hands on the weapon or limb, coupled with good forward movement (discussed in a later chapter), should get us safely past stages 1 and 2 above, but we want to transition to proper Control or even past that before we get to stage 3 mentioned above.

"YOUR FIRST FIGHT IS FOR CONTROL, YOUR SECOND FIGHT IS TO FINISH."

After the Entry, all initial focus should be placed on gaining Control. We define Control as:

> *Neutralising the immediate threat through*
> *controlling its movement.*
>
> *Holloway, Schalk; Coleman, Gavin. The Maul: Preparing*
> *for the Chaos of Close Combatives (p. 76). Kindle Edition.*

It is only when Control has been established that we have truly contained the immediate risk of injury or death. It does not help to try and fight, detain, arrest, etc. before doing so as essentially we'll start to suffer a loss by way of attrition. A quick reminder that certain wounds and injuries are timers, that is, their effect isn't immediate but can very easily start compounding as the CCI progresses. Consider, as an example, a punctured lung. The practitioner might be able to continue in the moment, but start to develop respiratory complications seconds or minutes later. As such, our first goal should be to isolate the movement of the immediate threat and gain a tactically better position in which it'll be difficult for the opponent to regain initiative or cause more damage. Once Control has been locked in we should also be very careful not to fiddle with, or attempt to overly adapt that position, lest we create a hole through which the opponent can escape. This risk is more prevalent than many know: remember the opponent's brain is most probably going to be busy trying to escape Control. During this time his movement might be very dynamic and unpredictable. I've seen, time and again, how they slip out of a hole, purely by chance, that the practitioner inadvertently made.

I can't stress how important it is that one should be extremely wary of relinquishing Control. When working through a CCI, the process should be driven to conclusion, reaching each stage as one would a milestone in a race. First Assess, second Entry, third Control, then Takedown and/or Release, and lastly Finish. Disengaging, adapting, or retreating from any milestone should be rooted purely in tactical necessity. For example, if the Control position isn't allowing enough leverage to affect a Takedown due to biomechanical differences then yes, transition to a better Control position WHILST maintaining positive contact and keeping at least one hand on the problem. Or consider, for example, the practitioner developing a stability and proceeding balance issue whilst affecting a Takedown and they feel themselves falling as well: in this case we would teach the practitioner how to fully commit to their own fall and use that momentum to add extra force to the opponent's fall.

There are also specific issues arising when disengaging from Control positions. Reflect for a moment on the fact that most joint locks or weapon control positions rely on applying force to a joint: usually, but not always, bending the joint in a direction that's creating pain and might lead to damage should the force be increased. Once we start to disengage from Control, we essentially ease up on that force and, as such, lose the pain and damage potential that we were relying on for compliance.

When it comes to weapons we also need to consider the following: with most weapons the grip favours the handler. A previous instructor of mine used to jokingly say that Glock spends millions of dollars designing and redesigning their grips for better comfort, stability, and control. When we apply Control to a weapon it'll usually be a hasty position and on a part of the weapon that might not be ideal or designed as a point of grip. Frequently, the practitioner's ability to Control the weapon is related to him applying directional force, meaning, force that negates the effectivity of the handler's grip, to the weapon. Should we back off from Control, we essentially remove this directional force and give the opponent back their ideal grip.

A good Control position also has the benefit of making the opponent wear themselves out. Once Control has been established, specifically the type of Control that's neutralised the immediate threat, the practitioner has won some time, not a lot of time as he shouldn't be maintaining any stage for too long, but at least enough time to re-assess and consider the Takedown/Release through Finish stages should he need to. During this time you might find the opponent expending a lot of energy trying to get out of Control. If the Control is locked in properly this is very beneficial to the practitioner as it'll assist in wearing the opponent out. Please note this won't apply to all opponents: certain pain resistant, stimulant laden, and/or highly motivated opponents might fight on for a significant amount of time. However, it's important for the practitioner to understand that if the Control is solidly locked in, they can, and should if able, take a moment to assess and ensure they are continuing in as effective a way as possible.

Lastly, it's also interesting to note that if you lock onto your opponent at a very close range, and you manage to tie your whole body weight to him, he'll be severely restricted in terms of the amounts and types of force that he can generate. In this case, it'll be extremely difficult for him to generate significant striking, stripping, or shoving force. Bear in mind, though, that if he has an edged and pointed weapon he doesn't need significant force to injure. However, if you've properly tied your body weight to his, he'll have to contend with both your and his mass, and it'll slow him down and cost him a lot of energy to try and move well. It's only after you disengage or create a hole that he'll again be able to generate effective striking, stripping, or shoving force.

The benefits of first fighting for Control is hopefully evident. Always spend the time and energy to Control first, once Control has been locked in then you can better proceed to the next stages.

"KEEP MOVING FORWARD AT ALL TIMES."

Once the practitioner Enters and launches the attack it's imperative that they drive forward until the CCI is resolved. This is true both in the mental as well as the physical sense. Here is what is meant in the physical sense:

There needs to be an active and stable leg drive into the opponent at all times. By stable, I mean that the practitioner shouldn't be leaning overly much into the opponent; the practitioner should also avoid "running" forward with the opponent. Both of these misapplications will create stability (preceding balance) issues should the opponent suddenly change direction and/or apply force to the practitioner in the same direction as the practitioner's drive. Instead, the practitioner should be conditioned to maintain a well structured athletic posture, whilst simply driving forward and into the opponent.

The basic direction of movement should be left to the opponent; it's not that the practitioner should try and drive the opponent somewhere specific at this stage, it's simply that the practitioner should drive into the opponent and, as such, maintain the close range required to resolve the CCI. If the practitioner allows the opponent to retreat and disengage it won't be possible to apply any more combatives and, even worse, the CCI might need to be restarted from Entry. Obviously this will create risk as it unnecessarily extends the duration of the CCI and requires the practitioner to go through the timing and execution issues related to Entering a second time.

An extension of this principle relates to what we call Positive

Contact. The practitioner should, whether in terms of leg driving as described above, or whichever other contact based technique or procedure, be gently but firmly pushing forward and into the opponent at all times. There are two main reasons for this: first, the Positive Contact allows us to determine the immediate and next movement intention of the opponent faster than which sight can (kindly refer to The Maul Book for cited research indicating the significant reaction time differences between the tactile and visual sensory organs); second, it is safer and easier to transition between control options if we maintain consistent Positive Contact.

Each time we let go of a Control position, for whatsoever reason, we inadvertently open a hole through which the opponent can slip out and/or harm someone. The dynamism of the CCI here counts against the practitioner: if they let go at the wrong moment they'll lose the opponent and need to re-establish Control.

Lastly, one of the primary goals of forward movement is the practitioner's placement in relation to the weapon. The safest place to be is behind the weapon. This is true for both hot and cold weapon categories. Once we Enter and get hands on the weapon, or weapon-bearing limb, the instinctive response of the opponent will be to jerk the weapon or limb. This initial jerk is usually not a committed fully powered movement pattern, but it is a lightning fast movement pattern. As such, once we commit to action, we need to move forward to account for this first jerk as fast as possible. After this, if we allow the opponent the space and opportunity to do so, they might attempt more focused and powerful stripping movements to try and dislodge the weapon or limb. Continuous forward movement also assists in negating his ability to do so effectively as it allows no space for power generation or for backing the weapon or limb out from the Control position.

"NEVER ASSUME A REACTION OR RESPONSE."

Things your opponent won't always do:

• Turtle up. Closing up to cover their faces, head, and/or the rest of themselves.

• Disengage. Pull away, fall, run away, and/or try to escape.

• Attack with only the weapon limb. Not using the secondary arm to defend, control the range, grab onto, and/or control the practitioner.

• Perform a single strike. Do only one movement and allow you to do multiple movements.

• Stand still. Provide a stationary body or targets which you can aim for and work on.

Notice I say won't always do, meaning, they might actually do it. That is the extremely dynamic nature of violence - there are no guaranteed reactions or responses.

However, notice also if you will, all of the above reactions and responses actually make the trainee's job easier. They are slanted in the favour of the trainee. Let me give the industry the benefit of the doubt and say it's probably not being done purposefully, however, it definitely is being done.

Without noticing it, many training environments provide easier resistance patterns based off these very specific assumptions. This allows the trainee to have a much more comfortable training experience; training in this way is enjoyable, tends to have very fast and impressive movement patterns, and adds much confidence to the trainee. However, have a training opponent assault a trainee in a dedicated and relentless manner and all of a sudden nobody wants to come back to class. This, unfortunately, is the economics of commercial training. Let's put the rant aside, though.

This principle is intimately connected to the assessment principle: the practitioner should be taught how to assess continuously rather than work off assumptions. Yes, during the incident we should be managing and driving the incident to our required outcome, but this is different than making assumptions; our ability to effectively drive a CCI is related to continuous assessment coupled with dynamic rapid decision making and competent technical execution, and not on making assumptions.

If, after applying force to an opponent, we get the expected outcome immediately, that's great. We then assess it as such and finish the process based on the desired outcome. However, it is a decision we make based on observed and interpreted data. The moment we make procedural decisions based on assumptions we place ourselves and our teams at great risk.

Assumption based decision chains will derail the moment that the opponent does not react or respond in the expected manner.

This can cause blind spots in the practitioner's conduct, causing them to miss certain key data and to be severely hurt or injured as a result. It will also slow down their reaction and response times as they have pre-committed themselves to ineffectual techniques and procedures. Lastly, it can interrupt the practitioner's own assessment and decision making processes to the extent that they lose initiative.

It is okay to anticipate and possibly expect certain reactions or responses, but we can never assume them.

"THE GOAL OF FORCE APPLICATION IS COMPLIANCE."

Any time that we need to move the CCI further along the process, and we meet a resistant or combative opponent, we should immediately apply the necessary force required to gain compliance.

Conversely, if an opponent, within the moment, is not resisting or being combative, we would arguably be able to either not apply any force, or at least, apply less force than with the resistant or combative opponent.

This means that the application of force is purely dependant on the resistance and combativeness of the opponent. Force application is thus dynamic. A practitioner should be conditioned on two things: one, that should they meet a resistant or combative opponent, to deliver force immediately or as fast as possible and in a decisive manner; and two, to regulate the amount of force applied based solely on what is required to gain compliance within that moment.

Consider, as example, having applied a shoulder lock to a standing opponent in the Control stage of resolving a CCI. Our next step would be to affect a Takedown. If I can transition from Control to Takedown immediately, I should do so. If the opponent is highly resistant or combative, and I'm not able to apply the Takedown, I should immediately use whatever combative technique I have in my toolbox, that would be efficient and effective within the moment, to interrupt or subvert the opponent's resistance. The moment that the combative technique accomplishes this I should affect the Takedown.

Getting back to the practicalities of the example: imagine standing behind the opponent and controlling him with a well locked shoulder. A quick instep kick to the back of the knee, a forward knee into the base of the spine, or even applying significantly more force into the shoulder lock, might all provide the interrupt required to successfully transition to the Takedown.

If one of the above three options gains compliance, no extra force application is required. This is what we call Appropriate Force. There is no need for the practitioner to strike the opponent more than what is required, there is also no need for the practitioner's ego to get in the way. For the professional, at least, force application is not personal: it is merely a tool used to gain compliance as we work towards the outcome we require.

On a personal note, I will add the following: I have done significant damage to others on both sides of the law. There are times, from later in my life, where I can justify the use of force. There are many times, from earlier in my life, where I used force for no justifiable reason. Speaking plainly: I hurt people out of maliciousness - pure and simple.

Apart from the fact that any damaging or killing of other human beings have tremendous emotional, psychological, and spiritual repercussions, I can wholeheartedly say that I sleep better when I'm confident that I was justified in hurting or damaging the other person, and even more so when I know that I didn't use more force than I truly needed to. This does not mean I would flinch when I need to apply force, that I'm weak, or that I'll be slow or soft in the moment. As I get older I've simply realised and embraced the responsibility of respecting life and only doing the damage that I truly need to. As I said, I sleep better being able to honestly evaluate my actions and know that I acted as correctly as I could in that moment.

"ROBUST AND POWERFUL TECHNIQUES SHOULD BE FAVOURED."

When we refer to techniques as being robust we mean to say that they should be applicable in a wide variety of situations.

There are literally hundreds of ways to strike, control, or take an opponent down. However, upon closer inspection, one should notice that many of those techniques are very technical and/or specialised (applicable within very specific types of situations). Considering the primary contexts of combatives, and the fact that limited training time is usually part and parcel of those contexts, it doesn't help to waste precious training time on overly difficult or specialised techniques. It makes significantly more sense to spend time on easier techniques that serve a broad range of situational or positional variations. Internally (meaning when I present training) we refer to the concept of Volume of Repetition (sometimes unaffectionately called donkey-work by ourselves and our clients).

Volume of Repetition is an important part of our training methodology - we aim to get as much repetition as possible, specifically within dynamic and unscripted practice drills. This requires a compact technique set, focusing rather on their successful application within a broad base of variation, than having a big bag of tricks that only get used occasionally.

One of the challenges that commercial training environments face (I've been there and am talking from experience) is that of "new material." Clients easily get addicted to learning new tricks and techniques, which forces the system or instructors to have to continuously generate new material. It's a feedback loop that eventually waters a system down and turns it into a low quality and ineffectual approach. These systems usually thrive in environments where the system is not actually tested in operation or within more severe self defense needs (meaning, where there's actual risk of SBH/GBH [severe or grievous bodily harm] or death). Unfortunately, the client doesn't realise that it's ineffective and remains entertained as long as they can learn something new. We need to resist this pattern, focus on selecting robust techniques, and then slant our training environments to condition these techniques against violent, dynamic, and sustained assault patterns.

In this same manner, the techniques we select should be able to deliver very high amounts of force with minimal complication of movement. If we have to pick one technique from two: we should pick the one that has the most potential for power generation with the least amount of finesse. Seeing as we only want to use the technique to gain compliance, it stands to reason that we should pick the ones with the highest probability of success in the shortest amount of training and execution time. Most frequently, this probability of success is directly related to the amount of force we can deliver into an opponent within the moment. As such, we should stop wasting our time with weak and fancy techniques. We're only going to apply the force when it's needed, so when we are forced to use it it should be able to accomplish the job immediately.

Usually, when it comes to our technique toolbox, we only need a single, powerful technique that works within a specific range and via a specific trajectory of movement. Due to the dynamic nature of violence, if any compromise in terms of technique adoption needs to be struck, then we might sacrifice slightly in terms of power generation to favour simplicity (think picking a low round house kick rather than a low spinning round house kick), but this would be the only valid reason to compromise.

Lastly, techniques should also be selected for their ability to shorten the CCI resolution process. That means we want to select

Entries that can immediately knock the opponent down and out if required; our Control positions need to be able to do significant damage through small increases in force should we need them to; the Takedowns should provide maximum impact of the opponent to the floor after affecting them. We should then take this toolbox of techniques and refine them one step further: by being thoughtful about only selecting and including techniques that feed into and from each other, allowing us to take shortcuts through the process when applied optimally.

"DON'T JERK-OFF IN MY CLASS."

This principle flows directly from the previous one and is related to the actual execution of power generation within training, practice, or actual use. I could easily have added it above but it gets shouted so much in our training spaces that it's worth its own short mention.

Jerking-off, within our training environments, is defined as any technique pattern which lacks the elements required to effectively generate force. Range, body movement, structure, any or all of these (see Schalk's Little Book on Fundamentals), might be missing from the movement pattern, essentially rendering the technique useless. The term stems from our frequent use of hammer fists. A hammer fist, delivered without good power generation, turns from a large and powerful gross motor movement into a small and fast movement pattern that resembles jerking-off. You will frequently notice how a single hammer fist, devoid of proper force generation, turns into three or four jerking-off movements; I've even noticed how, in some systems, it gets accompanied by this weird uttering of "tsh, tsh, tsh," or "dish, dish, dish," and so forth.

The term jerking-off is also effective from a trainee management point of view: no one wants to be seen as the guy or girl jerking-off in class. So when an instructor shouts at you, from across the room, "hey Schalk, stop jerking-off in my class," there is a unique motivation for them to stop as fast as possible. In essence then, we use this principle to interrupt the trainee's ineffectual force generation pattern as fast and bluntly as possible.

"RETAIN INITIATIVE AT ALL TIMES."

Initiative, within the context of CCIs, can be defined as being one or multiple steps ahead of your opponent with the goal of remaining in control of the incident. When I have initiative I am driving the CCI in the direction that I want to. I am acting, reacting, and/or responding, in such a way that I am ensuring the outcome that I desire. Even though there might be fluctuations in terms of who's dealing damage, who's initiating certain techniques, movements, or processes within the moment, ultimately I am doing what is necessary to remain in control of the process itself.

The scope of this initiative, and control, pertains to more than just physical engagement. For starters, it relates to the practitioner's personal mental processes. Consider the earlier discussion on the question of "when we enter." Whether considering an entry or follow up technique, verbal or physical boundary setting, or any form of verbal action or response for that matter, our goal should always be to remain one step ahead of the opponent. We should actively be considering scenarios and response options, setting triggers and priming ourselves, throughout the entire incident. The moment that the opponent interrupts our mental processes they have essentially stolen initiative and control from us. This does not mean that we cannot re-gain initiative or re-establish control, however, we would now need to expend resources (time and energy) to do so.

Furthermore, it also relates to any verbal engagement woven through the incident. There's a self-defense and combative industry term that's called "verbal judo." There's much good literature on this and a discussion on tactics and techniques within "verbal judo" is outside the scope of this book. It's important to reflect, though, that the use of good communication skills is equally important to retaining initiative and control of any situation. Many a volatile situation goes off the rails due to bad management of pre-incident communication.

It's also important to understand that many opponents will use verbal engagement to distract, escalate, and/or prepare themselves for a physical engagement. In certain environments the verbal engagement even gets used as a tool to judge the quality of the practitioner. If the practitioner loses control of the situation due to a lack of verbal management skills, the opponent will mark this as a sign of weakness and possible opportunity. This can lead the opponent to a posture of contempt over the trainee, as well as provide them with confidence that they can attack and will probably be successful if they do so.

It is unfortunate that, apart from pre-emptive striking, we don't see much training to this effect in the broader industry. Internally, we have specific boundary enforcement drills, both verbal and physical, that we incorporate into our training where we simulate the practitioner starting to lose control of a situation. We then teach skills on how to assess and regain initiative as fast as possible, and we spend time coaching and developing these skills in our clients.

A client needs to be able to recognise when they are starting to lose initiative and/or control, as well as be able to increase their forcefulness to the appropriate level needed to re-establish initiative and control. Whereas this is a sorely required ability for all practitioners, it is especially necessary for professionals: law enforcement, police, and security all have to file post incident reports and it is my contention that we should structure training in such a way as to compliment their ability to debrief, structure, and verbalise their actions in a coherent and sensible manner. It should also make sense that, if training is structured in this manner, it would assist the civilian self-defender to better justify their decisions and actions post-incident.

"EVERYTHING HAS TO SURVIVE PRESSURE TESTING."

The aim with pressure testing is to assess whether the correct mental and movement patterns have been ingrained into System 1. The mechanism for doing so is simulating actual CCI complexity, dynamism, and biometrics. We do so by adding different types of load to the practitioner: the main types of load are mental (situational complexity and incoming emotional variation and intensity), dynamism (speed of incoming information and unscripted elements), and metabolic (biometrics, significant increases in heart and respiration rates).

As we increase the load the trainee's brain will involuntarily switch to System 1: here we need to coach them into being able to switch back to System 2 until System 1 is needed, and then on when and how to let System 1 off the leash only once they have decided to do so, or when the situation demands it. I cannot overstate the importance of this: we need to understand that System 1 will attempt to take over when there is severe risk. We want to capitalise on System 1's tremendous boost to speed and gross motor strength, but we need to be extremely wary of its timing and probability issues. As previously discussed, when we Enter is extremely important; Entering too early carries various complications including but not limited to possible legal repercussions, unnecessary or untimely escalation of the incident, displaying your intention and/or weapon too early, or simply pissing the opponent off.

System 1 is prone to acting when it wants to, not necessarily when you want it to. This means that we need to condition ourselves to remain in System 2 until we decide to let the switch occur. We teach our clients correct self-management tools with which to do so, the most important of these being respiratory management (or breathing techniques) and cognitive (System 2) decision making whilst under pressure.

Breathing, heart rate, and emotional states are intimately and physiologically linked. By controlling breathing we can control the other two. We place a large emphasis then on two dynamics: getting and keeping breathing under control, and then picking the Moment of Execution of the Entry. On a practical level, an instructor will be moving around the floor and calling the trainee's out on both of these elements: verbally instructing them to "fix your breathing" and "you pick your moment."

As we add load, the practitioner will either successfully accomplish what they intended to, or a breakdown in process will occur.

DID YOU ENJOY
THIS BOOK?

The best way to thank an author for writing a book you enjoyed is to leave an honest review! If you are reading on paper you can do so by heading back to the page you purchased this book from. Alternatively, select the link below to post your review of 'Schalk's Little Book of Combative Principles'.

Thank you so much for taking the time to let other readers know what you thought of my book!

(PS. I sincerely love photos of books - and photos of my own books all the more! :D If you have any feel free to share one with me on social media; I'll be sure to post it and then credit you!)

Click here to review.

FOLLOW SCHALK TO
KEEP UPDATED

facebook.com/schalkhollowayauthor

instagram.com/schalkhollowayauthor

amazon.com/author/schalkholloway

www.schalkholloway.com

Schalk is a South African author known for The Maul Book, Schalk's Little Book Series, and Die Groot Storie. Schalk started his career as novelist in 2022 after suffering and recovering from a serious injury. His first novels, the Brooklyn Saga, drew inspiration from the years that he ran interventions in that tiny Cape Town suburb.

Schalk's professional background lies in Christian ministry, combatives and firearms instruction, as well as tactical and intelligence based operations in select security and policing environments (references available upon request).

OTHER BOOKS BY SCHALK

(AS FOUND ON AMAZON)

NOVELS

The Brooklyn Saga:

Disciple's Fault
Brother's Request

SUBJECT LITERATURE

The Maul Book (co-authored with Gavin Coleman)

The Little Book Series:

Schalk's Little Book on Fundamentals (The Black Book)
Schalk's Little Book of Combative Principles (The White Book)
Schalk's Little Book for Brothers (The Red Book)

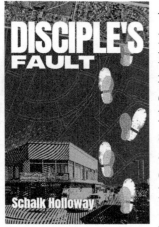

Disciple's Fault on Amazon

Frank Night is a lay minister that spends all his free time running interventions in at-risk communities. When the tiny community of Brooklyn, Cape Town, offers him two new cases, an unconventional stabbing leading to the death of a local boy, and a self-mutilating girl that disappears one Saturday night, he suddenly finds himself with much to do and manage.

A diagnosed neuro-divergent, his interactions with others are strained and complex at the best of times. But when the stress from these two interventions, as well as what seems like a neighbourhood that's set itself against him, starts to mount, he finally loses control. Just for an instant he becomes the man he used to be. Unfortunately for them, that single misstep places his wife firmly in the crosshairs of one of the local monsters.

REVIEW:

"Schalk's background gives him a huge edge when it comes to details and visualizations. The story is incredible and though written like a novel I get subtle hints that most of this book was written with experience. This is a great read and gives you a small slice of the pie in the combative world and life in Cape Town." - Loni Young

Brother's Request on Amazon

It's a couple of months after that disturbing night in Brooklyn. Frank and Didi have just started settling down but Brooklyn and the community's at it again: Jenny brings over a silent and highly detached friend, a new prostitute starts working their corner, and whereas Hamma's eventually finding his feet, certain interactions between him and the community has Frank concerned.

As if all of that isn't enough, even while Frank's trying to manage his neuro-divergence, he's also realising that he might slowly be losing control. Half the time he can't sleep due to nightmares and the other half is dominated by his recurring flashbacks. To complicate matters even further: a ghost from his past arrives in the neighbourhood.

A formidable man, and one that he used to call brother.

The Maul Book on Amazon

Did you know that the latest technology and research shows that the brain undergoes very specific changes in its functioning during a close combat incident? Whether training for self defence, law enforcement / military close combat procedures, or traditional martial arts and sports fighting - under certain conditions the brain will switch from one mode of functioning to another. The Maul Book is the first book to delve into this research, and through extensive testing within different close combat environments, integrate this research into new and fresh training methodologies. The Maul book is a must for any practitioner from any martial arts, self defence, close combat or tactical environment, as well as for instructors serious about providing the best training developed and influenced through the latest research.

Here's what you will learn from The Maul Book:

• What the latest research teaches on the brain's functioning under certain conditions.

• Old brain models that have now been shown as defunct and obsolete.

• How the changes in brain function influences performance and decision making within highly dynamic environments.

• How to better identify and select targets within high speed and ever changing situations.

• Techniques, tactics and training methodologies that work WITH the brain and its different ways of functioning.

• How to apply this research into any martial art or close combat training system.

• The core knowledge base of The Maul as an example of how to integrate the research into an existing system.

REVIEWS:

"I could easily just state that this is one of the best books on knife combatives I have read, ever, and be done with it. But that would be a disservice to both the authors and to you, the reader... It is, quite simply, the best approach to realistic knife combatives written in years... I cannot give it a higher recommendation than this, read it, practice it, read it again, and keep working it. This is good stuff. I wish this book was out when I started in this arena." - Terry Trahan

"The Maul tells you why some things probably won't work and why you should reassess your own training to realign it with what is currently known about the human brain. This is the most important book on Defensive Edged Weapons to come out in years." - Don Rearic

Schalk's Little Book on Fundamentals on Amazon

Striking and take-downs are the two primary tools in the martial arts or combatives practitioners arsenal. However, when we do not understand the fundamentals behind these tools they inevitably degenerate - strikes become less and less powerful and takedowns are ineffective and easily resisted or countered.

In this Little Book:

• How all take-downs fundamentally work and how to fix take-downs that aren't effective.

• How you can perfect your own take-downs as well as identify which take-down to apply to an opponent and when.

• How to generate the maximal amount of force in your strikes.

• How to ensure that the force generated is actually applied to your opponent.

• How to stop the generated force from bleeding or dissipating before making contact with your opponent.

And herein lies the purpose of this little book on Fundamentals. It is little in the sense that it means to offer a concise, easy to study and easy to assimilate, treatment on the topic of Fundamentals. Its aim, with a laser like focus, is on educating both the practitioner and instructor with the Fundamentals pertaining specifically to combatives and martial arts. Its goal is to assist the reader to not only sharpen up, but rather to excel, in all aspects of their fighting career.

The "Schalk's Little Book Series" is a collection of concise treatments on certain martial arts and combative related themes and topics. All the books are just under 10 000 words in length and purposefully designed to be easily digested and referenced.

REVIEW:

"I've had the privilege of being instructed by Schalk and assisting him instruct others over the years. He is one of the few people who are natural born teachers and has a remarkable ability to assimilate information and deliver it in a concise and easy to understand way. Even complicated technical subjects. This is what the Little Book of Fundamentals does. For someone like me who comes from a very informal Combatives background, I've always felt my understanding of fundamentals is lacking. A book like this goes a long way to patching up that fundamental information and gives some practical guides to troubleshooting any issues you may be having with takedowns or striking. A handy thing to have." - Gavin Coleman, co-author of The Maul Book and owner at Ironside Edgeworks

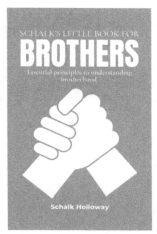

Schalk's Little Book for Brothers on Amazon

For many of us, the concept of brotherhood was entrenched (pun intended) in the literal and proverbial trenches.

Whether on the streets, in the military or other teams, or through the navigation of large societal chaos or deep personal adversity, a relationship was tested by fire and found to be gold: men, or women, were brought together, almost as if destined or divinely appointed, to face life, death, and all the tragic adversity in between, together.

However, the word is complex: for some it means I've killed for you, or I've almost been killed for you, and I'll do it again; for others it stands almost next to nothing, an empty term, meaning no more than: 'Hey, you.'

This Little Book is an attempt to concisely unpack and highlight the principles that underlie true brotherhood. If it's successful it might help some of us understand the word in a more healthy and balanced manner, and it might help some others, at the very least, to be more careful when they use the word, but hopefully, to know that when they do use it, that it should actually mean something.

The "Schalk's Little Book Series" is a collection of concise treatments on certain martial arts and combative related themes and topics. All the books are just under 10 000 words in length and purposefully designed to be easily digested and referenced.

Printed in Great Britain
by Amazon

19456399R00041